JESUS | Is He really the
only way?

JESUS - Is He really the only way?
ISBN: 978-1-933433-15-8

■

Copyright © 2008 Beth Ann Jones

Published by Beth Jones Ministries
2500 Vincent Dr., Portage, MI 49024
800-596-0379 bethjones.org

Printed in the United States of America.
ALL RIGHTS RESERVED.

■

JESUS | Is He really the
only way?

Contents

Find The Chapter

Chapter One

■ Who Says Jesus Is The Only Way?

How can you Christians be so narrow-minded and intolerant? What about other religions? What about Buddha? Mohammed? Confucius? Spirituality? There are many ways to God...so, why do Christians say that Jesus is the only way?

> *Lots of people ask these questions.*
> *I did.*

From news anchors, politicians, financial power-brokers and the academic elite to the local barista, grocery store cashier and man on the street,

Jesus has been believed, received, exalted and worshipped or bashed, ignored, belittled and dismissed. One way or the other, people have an opinion about Jesus, God, the Bible and faith.

■ Survey Says

Interestingly, a recent study showed that the majority of Americans are very open in their views about faith. Is that a good thing? A politically correct thing? A tolerance thing? A dangerous thing?

A major survey by the Pew Research Center's Forum on Religion & Public Life finds that most Americans have a non-dogmatic approach to faith. Their findings stated,

> *"A majority of those who are affiliated with a religion, for instance, do not believe their religion is the only way to salvation and*

almost the same number believes that there
is more than one true way to interpret the
teachings of their religion. This openness to a
range of religious viewpoints is in line with the
great diversity of religious affiliation, belief and
practice that exists in the United States, as
documented in a survey of more than 35,000
Americans that comprehensively examines
the country's religious landscape."[1]

Seventy-percent of respondents said that *"many*
religions can lead to eternal life."[2]

The survey went on to report,

"Most Americans agree with the statement
that many religions—not just their own—can
lead to eternal life. Among those who are
affiliated with a religious tradition, seven-in-
ten say many religions can lead to eternal
life. This view is shared by a majority of

adherents in nearly all religious traditions, including more than half of members of evangelical Protestant churches (57%). Only among Mormons (57%) and Jehovah's Witnesses (80%) do majorities say that their own religion is the one true faith leading to eternal life."[3]

The USA Today reports, *"Religion today in the USA is a salad bar where people heap on upbeat beliefs they like and often leave the veggies—like strict doctrines—behind."*[4]

It's clear that in our current culture, where more than 70% of the population claims to be Christian, we have a mixed bag of faith. People are becoming more and more "vanilla" and less and less dogmatic in their faith persuasions. The idea that a person would believe in Jesus as the only way to God and eternal life is becoming a foreign concept.

As published by the New York Times, *"It's not that Americans don't believe in anything,"* said Michael Lindsay, assistant director of the Center on Race, Religion and Urban Life at Rice University. *"It's that we believe in everything. We aren't religious purists or dogmatists."*[5]

Is believing in "everything" a good thing—eternally? In light of the spiritual climate these days, and as believers in Jesus, it's even more important that we know what we actually believe and why. Who is Jesus and what's the big deal about His life, ministry, death and resurrection?

▌ Ground Rules

Why does Jesus matter? What makes Jesus so different? What makes Him stand apart from other religious leaders? What makes His statements so unique and why are His true followers so passionate about Him?

Before we dive into that discussion, let's look at a fundamental reality that should set the tone for any conversation about God, faith or religion.

Respect.

Fortunately, we live in a country that values freedom of religion. Every person is entitled to hold to his or her own spiritual, religious or faith-based beliefs. This is not true around the world. We have the freedom to choose, without forcing or imposing our beliefs on others. This is a great luxury and benefit to every religion.

This is God's nature.

God is pro-choice! God Himself gives us freedom to choose. He doesn't force us to believe. As long as a person's belief system is not immoral, unethical, illegal or inhuman, we owe each person the respect they deserve to make his or her own faith choice. These are basic ground rules.

At the same time, while we respect the beliefs of others, there is nothing wrong with being passionate and persuasive about your own faith. In fact, it's advised! We ought to believe what we believe. We ought to know what we believe and why. We should be able to give an intelligent, gentle and respectful answer to someone who asks us about our faith.

"But in your hearts set apart Christ as Lord. **Always be prepared to give an answer to everyone who asks you** *to give the reason for the hope that you have. But* **do this with gentleness and respect***,"* (1 Peter 3:15, NIV).

We ought to have a strong foundation for our faith and deep convictions for what we believe, and we ought to be compelled by God's love to persuade others. *"It's no light thing to know that we'll all one day stand in that place of judgment.* **That's why we work urgently with everyone we meet to get them ready to face God.** *God alone knows how well we do this, but* **I hope you realize how much and deeply we care***,"* (2 Corinthians 5:11-12, MSG).

With these ground rules in mind, whatever your reference point happens to be, I am hopeful that you will take time to explore and consider this respectful and passionate response to the common question, *"Jesus: Is He really the only way?"*

■ Big Claim

Let's start with a big claim.

What is the difference between Jesus and...

Buddha?

Confucius?

Mohammad?

Hindu gods?

New age icons?

The spiritual world?

The spirit in man?

Any religious leader?

The difference between Jesus and other religious leaders or icons is summarized in one of the claims that He made about Himself. Jesus made a big claim. It all starts here.

Jesus said, *"I am the way, the truth, and the life. No one comes to the Father except through Me,"* (John 14:6, NKJV).

This is huge! Notice, He didn't claim to be *a* way or *a* truth or *a* life; rather Jesus claimed to be *the* way, *the* truth and *the* life. He made this distinction crystal clear when He stated that *"No one comes to the Father except through Me."* This is a very dogmatic claim and it makes all the difference. Did Jesus tell the truth?

Jesus didn't suggest that He was just a prophet or religious teacher, He claimed to be God. This is dramatic and we are forced to deal with His claim.

It's all about John 14:6.

C.S. Lewis, an Oxford and Cambridge professor and renowned author, said, *"You must make your choice. Either this man was, and is, the Son of God, or else a madman or something worse. You can shut Him up for a fool, you can spit at Him and kill Him as a demon, or you can fall at His feet and call Him Lord and God. But let us not come with any patronizing nonsense about His being a great human teacher. He has not left that open to us. He did not intend to."*[6]

Our response to His claims has major ramifications that are life-changing. This often makes people uncomfortable and the easy reaction is to be "all-inclusive" or "anti-Christ" about the whole religion thing.

Why all the fuss?

■ Is This An Anti-Christ Culture?

We've discussed the "all-inclusive" attitude a bit, but let's look at the "anti-Christ" perspective. In our global culture and liberal media, it's become perfectly acceptable to diss Jesus, the Bible and Christianity, but intolerable for anyone to make disparaging remarks about other religious leaders or their holy books. Why the apparent inconsistency?

The bottom line? People struggle with absolutes and they prefer relativism. Many people reject the idea of absolute right and wrong, but rather embrace a relativistic "whatever-works-for-you" attitude. The interesting thing is that most relativistic thinkers would never apply their ideals to their favorite sports team or early morning traffic. Can you imagine the chaos?

This "whatever-works-for-you" way of thinking doesn't work in real life. For example, what if I don't believe in absolute red lights? What if I believe that when the light is red, it works better for me to *go*? If red means *stop* to you, then by all means stop. If red means *go* to me, then I have to live by my beliefs. Can you see how ridiculous this way of thinking can be in areas that are absolute?

People don't like absolutes. They especially don't like Jesus' bold absolute claim that He is the *only way* to God the Father.

Why?

Unbelievers can't imagine God being so absolute and narrow-minded as to make Jesus the only door of entrance into God's kingdom. Often, this is because they don't really understand who Jesus is, *what the point is*, or why He came and their bias prevents them from listening.

Believers can't understand why anyone would be so tied to relativism as to reject God's generous gift and close the door of their hearts to Jesus Christ. Often, believers have not done a very good job of sharing Christ in word or deed; and they wonder why unbelievers are so hostile to everything related to Jesus.

Case in point: in most schools and public places, you can celebrate Halloween, Kwanzaa, Hanukkah or a host of other religious events, but the minute someone wants to celebrate Christmas or Easter, there is a bias against Jesus. Santa and the Easter Bunny are invited, but baby Jesus is not. What is it about Jesus that sets people off? His absolute claims.

Jesus is not politically correct.

In an odd sort of way, doesn't all the anti-Christ propaganda and Jesus-bias behavior around the world serve as proof for the very veracity of Jesus?

Think about it. People have no problem talking about God, angels, spiritual things, other religious leaders—even prayer—but when you start talking about Jesus, the room gets uncomfortably silent or noticeably agitated. His Name has either blessed or irritated people since New Testament times. It's nothing new.

■ The Swear Word Test

Here's an interesting experiment. Prove for yourself that Jesus is unique and holds the absolute Name above all names.

Take the Swear Word Test! (I don't actually recommend this, but it does make the point.)

The Swear Word Test.

Slam your toe into a brick wall or smash your thumb with a hammer. What words are you very tempted to say?

When people are really ticked off and they want

to use swear words with power, what words do they choose? It's not the godly thing to do, but whose name do they use in vain?

You know the swear words. When someone stubs their toe, they exclaim, *"Jesus Christ!"* sometimes followed up with other curses of God. Why? Because His name has power! Have you ever wondered why people don't swear by saying, *"Oh, Buddha!"*? When was the last time you walked down the street and heard someone cussing at a driver by saying, *"Oh Dalai Lama..."* or *"Confucius?"*

The reason you've never heard anyone use those names in vain is simple. Jesus is *the* Name with power—the Name above all names! When people want to use an expletive with power, when they want to curse or blame God for their pain, they innately use God's Name in vain by saying,

"Jesus Christ!" That alone ought to be evidence that Jesus is in a class of His own, as God!

Why does all of this matter? Why can't we just lump Jesus in with all of the other spiritual leaders of history?

In A League Of His Own

Jesus Christ is in an entirely different league than any other person or any other religious leader who has ever lived.

The thing that puts Jesus in a category apart from every other person in history is His claim to be God! Jesus never claimed to be *just* a religious teacher, rabbi, prophet or spiritual leader; He claimed to be God and this puts Him in a class by Himself!

If indeed Jesus was God in human flesh, this difference gives His birth, life, words and death a weight that no other religious leader can claim. Jesus *was* and *is* God—or He was a deceptive, crazy man! At some point, every person has to decide what he or she believes about Jesus. Who is He? What did He say? Why was He here?

Who Is Jesus?

Jesus is not a theory. Religion. Concept. Ideology. Jesus is a person. Jesus is the fulfillment of God's redemptive plan and hundreds of prophecies.

The New Testament gospel accounts tell us about Jesus as the Son of God, the Son of Man, the Messiah and the Light of the world. He is known as a rabbi, great teacher, preacher, healer and miracle-worker who was full of truth, grace and compassion. He is called Savior, Lord, Redeemer, Lamb of God and the great "I AM."

The Bible says, *"Jesus Christ is the same yesterday, today, and forever,"* (Hebrews 13:8, NKJV). Millions of believers over the past 2,000 years will attest to that as they tell of their personal encounters with the living Jesus Christ. There is no doubt that His life changed human history.

"Before anything else existed, there was Christ, with God. He has always been alive and is Himself God. *He created everything there is—nothing exists that He didn't make.... And Christ became a human being and lived here on earth among us and was full of loving forgiveness and truth...***But although He made the world, the world didn't recognize Him when He came.** *Even in His own land and among His own people, the Jews, He was not accepted. Only a few would welcome and receive Him. But to all who received Him, He gave the right to become children of God. All they needed to do was to trust Him to save them."* (John 1:1-3, 14, 10-11, TLB)

Jesus claimed to be on a divine mission.

Jesus was here to save mankind! He wanted to rescue us from the enemy who had duped man since the Garden of Eden and He wanted to give us the abundant life He intended from the beginning.

*"**For this purpose** the Son of God was manifested, that **He might destroy the works of the devil**,"* (1 John 3:8, NKJV).

*"Jesus said, '**I have come that they may have life,** and that they may have it more abundantly,'"* (John 10:10, NKJV).

Jesus claimed to be the only way.

He didn't candy-coat it. He gave us the absolute truth. He made it plain.

"Jesus said, *'I am the way, the truth, and the life. No one comes to the Father except through Me,'*" (John 14:6, NKJV).

So, who is Jesus?

> *God with us?*
> *Liar? Liar?*

■ A Conversation

I'd like to share an interesting conversation that took place. I have a cousin who is quite bright, talented and spiritual. More than 25 years ago, she and I were corresponding about Jesus and whether He was really the only way to God. She couldn't imagine a loving God who was so narrow-minded as to make Jesus the *only way*. What about the other religions, she wondered?

I received a letter from her one day that ended up changing my life. She wrote me a note and asked one simple question.

One question.

"If God is so good and so loving, how could He crucify and murder His own Son—why the gory, bloody details?"

I thought she asked a good question. Somehow, I knew that the answer to this question would also answer the more important question that people ask, *"Is Jesus really the only way?"*

■ More Than Catechism

Like many people, at that time, I knew bits and pieces of what the Bible said about Jesus, His life and death on the cross. I remembered things I had learned growing up in church.

I knew the songs.
I knew the stories.

I knew the basics, *"For God so loved the world that He gave his only Son, so that everyone who believes in Him will not perish but have eternal life,"* (John 3:16, NLT).

In order to answer my cousin's question, I needed my understanding to be more than just catechism. As I set out to respond to her letter, I prayed. *"God, why **did** You send Your own Son to the cross? Didn't You have other options? Why the gory, bloody details? Why **is** Jesus the only way?"*

I remembered a phrase we had memorized and said in church each week, *"Lamb of God who takes away the sins of the world, have mercy on me...."* Why was Jesus being called a lamb and why did the *sins of the world* matter?

I prayed again.

*"Father, help! You know why Jesus is the only way;
You know why the gory, bloody details were neces-
sary. Why did Jesus have to die on a cross? Why is
Jesus the only way?"*

Let me share what I learned....

Chapter Two

■ Is This A State Of Emergency?

"Today, the world is a pretty distressing place. People are pretty much ... Self-absorbed. Money-hungry. Self-promoting. Stuck up. Profane. Contemptuous of parents. Crude. Coarse. Dog-eat-dog. Unbending. Slanderers. Impulsively wild. Savage. Cynical. Treacherous. Ruthless. Bloated windbags. Addicted to lust. **Allergic to God**,*"* (2 Timothy 3:1-2, MSG).

Thousands of years ago, the Bible predicted the times in which we live. Does the above passage describe our world or what? This wasn't God's original plan. He definitely had something better in mind.

In my search for an answer to my cousin's question, the Lord took me back to the beginning and His original plan. Let's take a journey....

■ The Original Plan

God's original plan started with Adam. Remember? God was the creative artist. He scooped up some dirt and sculpted a statue. He named this hunk of dirt Adam. Then, God did something amazing. He breathed the *breath of life* into Adam's nostrils and the Bible says this statue became a man—a living, moving, breathing person!

Talk about modern art.

Can you imagine that scene? A statue becomes a

living person! Genesis 2:7 says, *"...The LORD God formed the man from the dust of the ground and breathed into his nostrils **the breath of life,** and the man became a living being,"* (NIV).

God's breath filled Adam and he became a man full of the **life of God**—spirit, soul and body.

From Adam's rib, God formed Eve and put them both into a lush, life-filled garden to rule and reign. It was paradise! The Garden of Eden was loaded with fresh fruit, trees, rivers, and beauty and God gave them authority over all of it! Everything in God's original plan resounded with LIFE!

God's original plan was LIFE!

Genesis 1:26-28, *"Then God said, 'Let Us make man in Our image, according to Our likeness; let them have dominion over the fish of the sea, over the birds of the air, and over the cattle, over all the earth and over every creeping thing that creeps on the earth.' So God created man in His own image; in the image of God He created him; male and female He created them. Then* **God blessed them,** *and God said to them, 'Be fruitful and multiply; fill the earth and subdue it; have dominion over the fish of the sea, over the birds of the air, and over every living thing that moves on the earth,'"* (NKJV).

Life was good in the Garden.

The Lord's original plan was to saturate humanity with His LIFE. He gave us everything we needed—a free will, a sharp mind, rich abundance, a healthy body, authority, blessings, great interpersonal relationships—including a personal relationship with Him! He wanted to bless and prosper mankind with everything that life represented!

■ Life And Only Life

Life was everywhere! Adam, Eve and the Garden were loaded with the life of God.

Do you get the picture? God's goal and desire for mankind was LIFE—blessing, fruit, multiplication, authority and dominion. His original intent for mankind is summarized in this...

life, life, life, life, life, life!
life, life, life, life, life, life!

God never wanted death for mankind—He only wanted life. However, at the same time He imparted life, He gave man a free will with a few instructions.

"The LORD God placed the man in the Garden of

Eden to tend and care for it. But the LORD God gave him this warning: '**You may freely eat any fruit in the Garden except fruit from the tree of the knowledge of good and evil. If you eat of its fruit, you will surely die,**'" (Genesis 2:15-17, NLT).

▇ Death And Only Death

We all know the story. Adam and Eve broke the one rule. They disobeyed God's one command and ate from the tree of the knowledge of good and evil.

The result? Death. The Lord told them, *"...If you eat of its fruit, you will surely die,"* (Genesis 2:7, NLT). The day they ate of the fruit of that tree, they surely died.

Adam and Eve sinned and allowed "death" to enter into this perfect set-up. They listened to and obeyed the serpent—the devil—who tempted them through lies. They ate the forbidden fruit and death entered the human race and snuffed out the LIFE God had given them! The moment they sinned, two types of death entered.

Spiritual death.
Physical death.

First, they died spiritually and their hearts were separated from God. Second, they died physically and their bodies expired more than 900 years later.

Death became a major problem for mankind. The original plan was life, but after Adam and Eve sinned, death entered the human race.

This was cataclysmic. Tragic. Mankind went into a 911 code blue condition! This was a state of emergency. The whole human race suffered the day Adam and Eve sinned. Adam represented all mankind, and death entered the entire human race after Adam and Eve took a bite of the fruit!

It's spelled out in the Bible, *"When Adam sinned, sin entered the entire human race. **Adam's sin brought death, so death spread to everyone, for everyone sinned**,"* (Romans 5:12, NLT).

Death reigned. *"... By the trespass of the one man, **death reigned through that one man... through the disobedience of the one man the many were made sinners**,"* (Romans 5:17, 19, NIV). Death—separation from God—spread to all men.

■The Hole

Down through the ages, this spiritual death or separation from God created an internal aching void in all of us. Deep inside, every person knows he or she is created for a life with God! There is an empty hole in each of us and we know it.

We often try to fill that void *without* God. We try substitutes: addictions, money, status, relationships, material things, intellectualism, intoxication, parties, prestige and power—you name it. We always come up empty—never satisfied—because there *really* is a God-shaped hole caused by *death* lodged in all of us.

Up until "the fall," mankind had enjoyed a friendship with the Lord and lived life as God intended. However, the minute they ate the forbidden fruit they died, and there was a spiritual separation. Everything God made resounded **life, life, life**—and after the fall everything resembled **death, death, death.** Mankind needed supernatural life support.

God breathed life.

Adam and Eve sinned.

Death entered.

Houston, we have a problem.

Chapter Three

■ Can We Get A Do-Over?

Death seems so final. Bill was hit by a train and pronounced dead at 1 o'clock in the morning. My mom's boyfriend—young, strong and athletic— was dead.

I was 14 years old and couldn't accept it. I heard the news at 9 am and I ran to my bedroom where I cried out to the Lord from the depths of my being, *"God...no...bring him back!"* Don't ask me to explain this theologically—maybe God gave me the gift of faith on credit—all I know is that the hospital called the house a short time later to say that Bill had started to breathe on his own and mom better get up to the hospital!

Life overcame death!

Mankind was pronounced dead at the fall and God's heart cried out, *"I will bring you back!"* How could God reverse the curse of death? Was a do-over an option?

■ Do-Over?

Do you remember playing childhood games like, Tag, Hide-n-Seek, Crazy Eights, or Checkers?

Games were great when you were winning, but what did you call for the minute you lost? A "do-over!" If you didn't like losing, you simply called for a do-over.

There is no doubt that God didn't like the results of mankind's fall, so why didn't He call for a do-over?

What about Plan B? Plan C? Plan D?

Plan B? When Adam and Eve blew it in the Garden, why didn't God say, *"Adam and Eve, you blew it! There's obviously a flaw in the mold so, I'm going to call for a—do-over. I have to eliminate the two of you and start over."* Why didn't He just start from scratch after the big fall in the Garden? Why not just wipe out Adam and Eve and introduce two new humans—Ken and Barbie? After all, nobody would ever know! Why didn't God do that? He's God; can't He do anything He wants to do?

Plan C? If Plan B wasn't an option, why didn't God say, *"Adam and Eve, just say you're sorry—without* rolling your eyes! I'm going to snap My fingers and on the count of three, we're just going to call all this forgiven and forgotten." Why didn't Adam and Eve apologize and why didn't God just "snap His fingers" and fix it?

Plan D? If Plan B and Plan C wouldn't work, why didn't God say, *"Adam and Eve, you really messed things up for the rest of humanity! In order to reverse the curse of death, all mankind will have to become very religious and benevolent. If you pick a religion and do ten good deeds every week, I'll consider all sins paid for."*

Why couldn't God base the salvation of mankind on a do-over, snapping His fingers, religion or good deeds?

There's a reason...

There is a really profound, legal reason that God couldn't use Plan B, C or D! But before we look at that reason, do you concur that *if* God could have done anything other than send Jesus to the earth—where He would ultimately die on a cross and shed His blood—He would have done it?

If God could have used any other method for reversing "death," securing a relationship with humanity and providing eternal life for mankind, there is no doubt—He would have employed it!

Fortunately, before Adam and Eve sinned in the Garden, God already had the rescue plan in place. His *original plan* was—life, but He also had a *Master Plan* that went into effect the moment death entered.

Original Plan.
Master Plan.

■ Life Blood

What is the one thing that reverses death? There is only one thing that overcomes death—LIFE. Life triumphs over death!

When Adam and Eve fell and death entered the scene, God couldn't just provide knee-jerk, remedial solutions through Plan B, C or D.

No.

God had to do something legal, intentional and eternal—something that went to the core of mankind's problem. To say, "do-over", snap His fingers, or require religion or good works wouldn't provide life. To conquer death, God needed to find life and fortunately, He just happened to know where it was!

Leviticus 17:11 tells us where life is found, *"... For the **life** of any creature **is in its blood.** I have given you the blood so you can make atonement for your sins. **It is the blood, representing life,** that brings you atonement,"* (NLT). Summarized—*"life is in the blood."*

According to the Bible, the only place that life is found is in the blood. God needed a blood donor so He could impart life back into dead mankind! Can you see that?

> Death was the problem.
> Life overcomes death.
> Life is in the blood.

■ Quick Fix & Temporary Plan

Under the Old Covenant, God set up a system of blood sacrifices to provide forgiveness and life to His people.

Immediately after the fall of man, the Lord went to work locating blood! You can almost hear Him saying, *"Clear!"* as He grabs the paddles, locates blood and begins to impart life back to humanity.

The Passover, detailed in Exodus 12:2-13, typifies the power of shed blood to overcome death and impart life.

"From now on, this month will be the first month of the year for you. Announce to the whole community that on the tenth day of this month each family must **choose a lamb or a young goat for a sacrifice***...This animal must be a one-year-old male, either a sheep or a goat, with no physical defects. Take special care of these lambs until the evening of the fourteenth day of this first month. Then each family in the community must slaughter its lamb. They are to take some of the lamb's blood and smear it on the top and sides of the door frame of the house where*

the lamb will be eaten...this is the LORD's Passover...
The blood you have smeared on your doorposts will
serve as a sign. **When I see the blood, I will
pass over you. This plague of death will not
touch you**," (NLT). The blood of the innocent
lamb provided protection from death.

The life is in the blood!

Hebrews 9:22 says, "...Without the **shedding of
blood** there is no forgiveness," (NIV). The legal
route to life, forgiveness, restoration, redemption
and salvation is found in the *shedding* of blood!

In order to secure forgiveness each year under
Jewish Law and this system of animal sacrifices,
God required the high priest to go through an
extensive ceremonial cleansing ritual after which
the priest would be qualified and responsible for
slaying an innocent, unblemished animal—a bull,
a goat or a lamb. It was the responsibility of the

high priest to take the shed blood into God's most holy place—and sprinkle this blood on the mercy seat.

When this was done, an atonement—which means to pardon, to cancel or to forgive—was completed. This shed blood covered the sins of the people for one year. The life in the blood overcame the death brought on by sin. Each year this process had to be repeated.

This was a shadow of things to come.

For hundreds of years, God was pleased to accept the shed blood of bulls, goats, and lambs to atone for—or temporarily cover—man's sin and give life. Through the shedding of innocent blood, sins were covered and God's people were able to have a life-giving relationship with Him.

The sacrificial system under the Old Covenant was quite a process, but it was only a *temporary* solution. It was *temporary* blood, from *temporary* animals to *temporarily* cover sin and provide forgiveness and life. It was a good measure, but it wasn't God's permanent fix. It wasn't His ultimate plan. It wasn't his Master Plan.

In order to provide the *eternal* solution, God needed eternal, sinless blood.

Who could serve as a qualified donor for the eternal, sinless blood transfusion mankind required?

What was His Master Plan?

Chapter Four

■ What Is The Master's Plan?

Chess is a great, strategic, brain game. While you are making each move, you have to have a comprehensive plan in your mind. You must be thinking several moves ahead in order to win. If you want to say, *"Checkmate"* you need to have a smart Master Plan.

Down through the ages, with every move made, God was working His Master Plan! Checkmate would happen when He sent His one and only Son—Jesus Christ!

■ Brilliant!

God's Master Plan was brilliant! He was not satisfied with the *temporary* blood sacrifice of animals. His Master Plan would provide *permanent* forgiveness and eternal life through the eternal, sinless blood sacrifice!

Let's look at various scenarios to discover how God "found" the permanent, eternal and sinless blood option He needed. Who had the "blood type" God required? Who qualified? It seems that the Lord had four options for finding a blood donor match.

Blood types.

Type #1: Animals—Animals have blood, but their blood isn't eternal. Their temporal blood could not provide perfect, eternal cleansing.

Summary: Not a match.

Type #2: Man—Man is an eternal being and he has blood, but his blood was contaminated with death through sin.

Summary: Not a match.

Type #3: God—God is eternal and sinless, but He is a Spirit and doesn't have a physical body with blood.

Summary: Not a match.

Type #4: God/Man—If God, who is eternal and sinless, could become a human man with blood, this would provide the perfect eternal, sinless type of blood that is qualified to provide life.

Summary: Perfect match!

■ Merry Christmas!

The blood explains Christmas! God became a man and put on flesh so that eternal, sinless blood could flow through His veins! You know the story—although, perhaps you *don't* really know the story! Let's look at it with fresh eyes.

All during the Old Testament sacrifice rituals, God was working on a bigger plan—the Master Plan that He had prepared before the foundations of the world! At the appointed time, God sent His angel Gabriel to speak to a young teenager named Mary.

The angel said, *"Greetings, favored woman! The Lord is with you! ... Don't be frightened, Mary, for God has decided to bless you!* **You will become pregnant and have a Son, and you are to name Him Jesus.** *He will be very great and will be called the Son of the Most High,"* (Luke 1:28-32, NLT).

She had one question. *"Mary asked the angel, 'But how can I have a baby? I am a virgin.'"* Mary was told that the Holy Spirit would overshadow her; she would conceive and give birth to the Son of God. Her response was simply, *"I am the Lord's servant, and I am willing to accept whatever He wants. May everything you have said come true,"* (Luke 1:34-38, NLT).

God bless Mary! It's a good thing she wasn't some half-backslidden, rebellious teenager with an attitude. She knew the Lord and had a sweet, humble, and obedient spirit.

It happened, just as the angel said. Mary became pregnant with the God-Man. In her womb, she carried the most unique person in all of history— The Savior Of The World—a baby with eternal, sinless, life-giving blood in His veins! Think about the eternal weight of that pregnancy.

Spotless blood.

God, through Jesus Christ, was born of a virgin. He took on a body as a baby and came to His own people. His circulatory system carried the *only* blood that was eternal, sinless and full of the life that could set men free from death.

God's Master Plan was for **Jesus** to become a human being, with blood! He carried the eternal, sinless blood—the type of blood needed to forgive mankind and impart eternal life—once and for all. The life was in **His** blood!

God humbled Himself, put on flesh and came to the planet He made. *"**Though He was God, He did not demand and cling to His rights as God. He made himself nothing; He took the humble position of a slave and appeared in human form.** And in human form He obediently*

humbled Himself even further by dying a criminal's
death on a cross," (Philippians 2:6-9, NLT).

■ Supernatural Pregnancy

Let's look at this pregnancy in a little more detail
through God's eyes.

Mary's conception must have been quite an event
for heaven! Can you imagine what it was like for
heaven's host to watch that 9-month pregnancy?
I wonder what it was like for God the Father
as He watched this young lady carry The Savior
Of The World—The Lamb of God with life-giving
blood—in her womb?

The eternal significance is staggering. A young
woman carried a baby—*who had eternal, sinless
blood*—in her womb! The only blood that could
provide eternal life!

The only blood.

Think about that very first Christmas when Mary delivered the Deliverer! When Jesus was born—for the first time in all of history—there was a person on planet Earth who had eternal, sinless blood in His veins.

The potential for mankind's forgiveness and eternal life was entirely wrapped up in the blood that flowed in Jesus' body.

The Master Plan was unfolding.

God's wisdom and attention to detail is even more astounding. Let's look closely at the bloodline. To ensure that the blood of Jesus would not be contaminated by the blood of a human mother or father, God had a wonderful plan:

The Incarnation.

The Holy Spirit overshadowed Mary and caused her to conceive Jesus. Conveniently, God had already designed the human pregnancy process in such a way as to ensure that a baby's blood never touches the mother's blood. Thus, Jesus could have eternal, sinless blood in His veins while He was growing in the womb of Mary.

Those of you who have had babies know how this works. It's a remarkable thing—a pregnant woman, with a certain blood type, can carry and deliver a baby with a different blood type! The circulatory system of the baby is never connected, other than by the placenta, to the mom's. There are two totally separate circulatory systems, ensuring that the blood of the baby is never contaminated by the blood of the mother.

Wasn't that smart of God?

■ Jesus Was The Master's Plan

Jesus was God's Master Plan! For hundreds of years, God patiently worked His plan so that in the fullness of time, Jesus could arrive on the scene with the eternal, sinless blood that would redeem mankind! God didn't just want to "cover" our sins; He wanted to "erase" them! He wanted to eradicate the death which came through sin, once and for all, and recreate man according to His original plan—full of life! Jesus, who was one with the Father and the creator through whom all things were made, chose to humble Himself, step out of heaven and set aside His rights as God in order to become a human being with eternal, sinless blood.

He chose to live on earth for several decades while He demonstrated the Father's love in teaching, preaching and healing. All the while, Jesus knew that His ultimate goal was the cross—*"the shedding of His blood"*—so that mankind could be forgiven and filled with eternal life.

Hebrews 10:1-12 tells us about God's Master Plan: *"The old system in the law of Moses was only a shadow of the things to come, not the reality of the good things Christ has done for us.* **The sacrifices under the old system were repeated again and again, year after year, but they were never able to provide perfect cleansing for those who came to worship.** *If they could have provided perfect cleansing, the sacrifices would have stopped, for the worshipers would have been purified once for all time, and their feelings of guilt would have disappeared. But just the opposite happened. Those yearly sacrifices reminded them of their sins year after year.* **For it is not possible for the blood of bulls and goats to take away sins.** *That is why Christ, when He came into the world, said, 'You* did not want animal sacrifices and grain offerings. But You have given Me a body so that I may obey You. No, You were not pleased with animals burned on the altar or with other offerings for sin. Then I said, 'Look, I have come to do Your will, O God—Just as it is written about Me in the Scriptures.'

"Christ said, 'You did not want animal sacrifices or grain offerings or animals burned on the altar or other offerings for sin, nor were You pleased with them' (though they are required by the law of Moses). Then He added, 'Look, I have come to do Your will.' He cancels the first covenant in order to establish the second. **And what God wants is for us to be made holy by the sacrifice of the body of Jesus Christ once for all time. Under the old covenant, the priest stands before the altar day after day, offering sacrifices that can never take away sins. But our High Priest offered Himself to God as one sacrifice**

for sins, good for all time. *Then He sat down at the place of highest honor at God's right hand,"* (NLT).

For ages upon ages, God worked a Master Plan to send *"...the Lamb of God, which taketh away the sin of the world,"* (John 1:29).

Jesus is eternity's hero! He is the Lamb of God. He is our High Priest. He shed His blood once and for all. *"God has purchased our freedom with His blood and has forgiven all our sins,"* (Colossians 1:14, NLT). Amazing. This is why Jesus really is the only way to God and heaven!

The life is in the blood.

Chapter Five

■ How Do You Define A Hero?

Let's talk about a hero. Unfortunately, we live in a culture of celebrity worship. We worship movie stars, athletes, recording artists, musicians, the wealthy, successful and powerful.

The result is that we've been disappointed by these so-called heroes. Politicians addicted to sex. TV stars in rehab. Sports heroes on steroids. Preachers committing adultery. If you want to worship a real hero—someone who has done something truly heroic, worship Jesus—the truest of all heroes.

The general definition of a hero is: *a remarkably brave person or someone who has shown great courage or strength of character.*

Jesus is a hero.

The reason that followers of Jesus are so passionate about Him is simple: He is the only person in human history who overcame death with life...with His blood! It all happened on the cross.

■ Under Pressure

Jesus had the eternal blood that would save mankind, but having the blood wasn't enough! He had to shed that blood. Jesus had to live a sinless life and get to the Cross.

He had an enemy.

Satan didn't understand everything, but he could read the handwriting on the wall and he knew there was something eternally unique about Jesus. He wanted Jesus to blow it and disqualify His blood. Satan tempted Jesus to sin in every way—through the lust of the flesh, the lust of the eyes and the pride of life. Jesus resisted every temptation to sin and the pressure to quit.

He displayed great bravery, courage and strength of character in the face of extreme pressure— the type of pressure that would make everyone else crack.

Literally, Jesus carried the weight of the world as He overcame these three pressures.

Pressure #1: Temptation to Sin. Jesus, as a man, had to live a sinless life. If Jesus wasn't successful in living a sinless life, it wouldn't matter if He went to the cross because His eternal blood would be unacceptable! Jesus had to live a perfect life—as a man! Although He was 100% God in the flesh, the Bible tells us that He set aside His rights as

God and became a human being (Philippians 2). Everything He did on earth, He did as a man empowered by the Holy Spirit.

Legally, Jesus had to live a sinless life, as a man. If He ever sinned once, His blood would be disqualified and all humanity would be lost! He was criticized, rejected, persecuted and tempted to sin, just like you and me—but Jesus never sinned.

Pressure #2: Temptation to Live. Jesus had to die and *shed* His blood. He had to give up His life so that we could have life. If Jesus did not lay down His life on the cross—so that His eternal, sinless blood could be spilled—then all of humanity would be lost! Jesus knew that *"without the shedding of blood"* there is no forgiveness. Jesus couldn't bail out. He had to die in order to shed His blood! Jesus chose the cross.

Can you see the magnitude of this?

In the Garden of Gethsemane, Jesus had to lay down His will to do God's will. No one took His life, He laid it down freely.

The eternal destiny of every person—the generations behind us and the generations to come—hung in the balance through the decisions Jesus made.

Jesus made the choice to die on the cross so His blood could be shed!

Pressure #3: Temptation to Quit. Jesus was God's *only* Son and if Jesus wasn't successful, all was lost. If Jesus sinned or backed out from going to the cross, death would remain and mankind would be eternally separated from God.

If Jesus was not successful, there wasn't a backup plan! Jesus was not "one of the sons"— He was *the only* Son! Here's a conversation that never happened. God the Father *didn't* give Jesus this pep talk:

> "OK, Jesus, You're going to go first. Through the Incarnation You'll become the God-Man with the eternal blood that will save humanity. I want You to lay aside every advantage You have as God and do this whole thing as a man—a substitute. Now, do Your best, avoid sin and prepare Yourself for the crucifixion. If it doesn't work out, don't worry, I've got a contingency plan...I'll just send one of my other Sons ..."

There was no contingency plan. The Bible says that Jesus was the *only* begotten Son of the Father. *"For God so loved the world that He gave His **one and only Son,** that whoever believes in Him shall not perish but have eternal life,"* (John 3:16, NIV).

■ He Took Our Place On Purpose

Sometimes when we read the Bible, we don't realize the difficult decisions Jesus had to make as a man. Although He was God in the flesh, He laid aside every God advantage He had so that He could live as a man and be our legal substitute. He chose to resist every temptation, and shed His blood on the cross so that we could receive eternal life! He gave His life in exchange for ours. He, literally and legally, took our place! Why?

The thought of humanity being set free from the penalty of sin and death brought Jesus great joy. He endured the cross with us in mind. *"He was willing to die a shameful death on the cross because of **the joy** He knew would be His afterward,"* (Hebrews 12:2, NLT). The "joy" was us!

Jesus was motivated to shed His blood on the cross because He knew the joy that would be His as He redeemed mankind from sin and death into forgiveness and life with God!

Jesus was very intentional.

He said, *"No one can take My life from Me.* ***I lay down My life voluntarily. For I have the right to lay it down when I want to and also the power to take it again.*** *For My Father has given Me this command,"* (John 10:18, NLT).

When they arrested Jesus, He reiterated who was in control. *"Don't you realize that I could ask My Father for thousands of angels to protect us, and He would send them instantly? But if I did, how would the Scriptures be fulfilled that describe what must happen now?"* (Matthew 26:53-54, NLT).

Jesus could have bailed out at any time and angels would have rescued Him—instead, He chose to go to the cross on our behalf!

Jesus defines a hero!

■ It Wasn't Pretty

Remember this story in the Garden of Gethsemane?

"He told them, *'My soul is crushed with grief to the point of death. Stay here and watch with Me.'* He went on a little farther and fell face down on the ground, praying, **'My Father! If it is possible, let this cup of suffering be taken away from Me. Yet I want Your will, not Mine.'** ... Again He left them and prayed, *'My Father! If this cup cannot be taken away until I drink it, Your will be done,'*" (Matthew 26:38-43, NLT).

Jesus chose to drink the bitter cup! When He prayed in the Garden, perhaps in our modern language, the conversation would have sounded like this:

> *"Father, if there is any other way that You can do this—if there is any other way to provide mankind with forgiveness and eternal life, I beg You to show Me. If it's possible for You to consider a do-over, snapping Your fingers, or accepting world religions or good works as sufficient for redemption—please let this cup pass from Me. I don't want to go to the cross. I don't want to drink this cup. If there's any way I could avoid crucifixion, if I don't have to die and shed My blood—please Father, let it be. Nevertheless, I won't choose what I want; I choose Your will."*

Sometimes, we over-spiritualize Jesus' journey to the cross. Often we don't realize that He, in

His flesh, didn't *want* to be severely beaten. He didn't *want* to be spit at, kicked, mocked, whipped and brutalized to the point that He was not recognizable as a human being.

Jesus didn't float to the cross.

Everything about the human experience—our past, present and eternal future—hung on one event: the crucifixion!

The crucifixion is foolishness to many people these days: the wise, scholarly, philosophical, academic and religious among us. To others, the cross is God's hidden wisdom.

"Where is the wise man? Where is the scholar? Where is the philosopher of this age? Has not God made foolish the wisdom of the world? For since in the wisdom of God the world through its wisdom did not know Him, God was pleased through the

foolishness of what was preached to save those who believe. Jews demand miraculous signs and Greeks look for wisdom, but **we preach Christ crucified:** a stumbling block to Jews and foolishness to Gentiles, but to those whom God has called, both Jews and Greeks, Christ the power of God and the wisdom of God. **For the foolishness of God is wiser than man's wisdom,** and the weakness of God is stronger than man's strength," (1 Corinthians 1:20-25, NIV).

"For those who have ears to hear and eyes to see, it's easy to say, 'I resolved to know nothing while I was with you except **Jesus Christ and Him crucified**,'" (1 Corinthians 2:2, NIV).

"Jesus went to the cross. He gave His life. His blood was shed. In His last moments Jesus said, **'It is finished!'** Then He bowed His head and gave up His spirit," (John 19:30, NLT).

Mission accomplished.

He knew the weight of the world was on Him. The eternal destiny of mankind was in the balance as Jesus faced and overcame every challenge, every pressure and every temptation to quit.

■ No Film At Eleven

Jesus never starred in a movie. Never shot a 3-pointer. Never held a public office. Never lived in Beverly Hills. Never recorded a CD. Didn't have His own jet. He lived a sinless life. He went to the cross. He shed His blood.

He is a hero.

Chapter Six

■ What Happened Behind The Scenes?

So, what's the big deal? A guy was crucified. He wasn't the first person to die by such a hideous death.

Those watching with natural eyes see an innocent man beaten to a bloody pulp, hung on a cross by thugs. Sad, but so what? Those watching with spiritual eyes see something else.

In the **visible** world, He died a hideous death on the cross. In the **invisible,** spiritual world, what really happened?

On that visible cross, Jesus Christ became the invisible bridge between God and men! Something spiritual happened in the invisible realm.

■ Our Substitute

Most people saw Jesus as a bloody man on a tree; the eye of faith sees Jesus on the cross as our substitute. Jesus took our place. He was our substitute. What does that mean?

A substitute takes the place of another.

Think about it. In school, when the "sub" shows up, the regular teacher gets released from the classroom. Jesus, as our substitute, showed up on the cross and paid for our sins, so that we could be released.

Jesus, as our substitute, went to hell for three days so we wouldn't have to go there. Jesus, as our substitute, was raised from the dead, so we could be raised with Him!

Let's review. "...***The wages of sin is death, but the free gift of God is eternal life through Christ Jesus*** *our Lord,*" (Romans 6:23, NLT).

Sin requires a payment. God can't and won't wink at sin, but rather justice requires that a wage be paid for it. The wages of sin is death. That's what happened in the Garden of Eden with Adam and Eve. They sinned and death entered. Since then, we've all sinned and we owe the debt of death!

Jesus paid our debt! He took our place. He was our substitute on the cross and in hell. He died for our sins! He paid our wage and we got His gift.

> *He paid the price.*
> *We got the gift.*

Jesus was here, on purpose, on a mission: to rescue all of us from sin and death.

■ His Cross Was Our Cross

Jesus' birth, life, ministry, death and resurrection were predicted hundreds of years before He came on the scene. Listen to Isaiah's amazing, detailed forecast!

"Many were amazed when they saw Him—beaten and bloodied, so disfigured one would scarcely know He was a person...He was despised and rejected—a man of sorrows, acquainted with bitterest grief. We turned our backs on Him and looked the other way when He went by. He was despised, and we did not care. **Yet it was our weaknesses He carried; it was our sorrows that weighed Him down.** *And we thought His troubles were a punishment from God for His own sins!* **But He was wounded and crushed for our sins.** *He was beaten that*

we might have peace. He was whipped, and we were healed! All of us have strayed away like sheep. **We have left God's paths to follow our own. Yet the LORD laid on Him the guilt and sins of us all.** He was oppressed and treated harshly, yet He never said a word. He was led as a lamb to the slaughter. And as a sheep is silent before the shearers, He did not open his mouth ..."

"**But who among the people realized that He was dying for their sins—that He was suffering their punishment?** He had done no wrong, and He never deceived anyone. But He was buried like a criminal; He was put in a rich man's grave. But it was the LORD's good plan to crush Him and fill Him with grief. Yet when His life is made an offering for sin, He will have a multitude of children, many heirs. He will enjoy a long life, and the LORD's plan will prosper in His hands. When He sees all that is accomplished by His anguish, He will be satisfied. **And because of what He has**

experienced, my righteous servant will make it possible for many to be counted righteous, for He will bear all their sins. *I will give Him the honors of one who is mighty and great, because He exposed Himself to death. He was counted among those who were sinners.* **He bore the sins of many and interceded for sinners**," (Isaiah 52:14, 53:3-12, NLT).

The cross isn't just about a man who survived beatings, mockery and torture. The cross is about the man who made a decision in the...

Garden of Gethsemane

...to rescue mankind from the sin and eternal death that had plagued humanity since the...

Garden of Eden.

His cross was our cross; we deserved to be

punished for our own sins, but He took our place and we were crucified with Him. *"I have been crucified with Christ; it is no longer I who live, but Christ lives in me,"* (Galatians 2:20, NKJV).

■ The Grand Finale

After His death on the cross, Jesus went to hell for three days—again, as our substitute! On the third day, He rose from the dead! This puts Jesus in a class all by Himself.

He's alive today!

One of the first things Jesus did after the resurrection was to take His own blood into heaven's most holy place, where He poured it out on the eternal mercy seat for the salvation of mankind! He is our eternal high priest.

"But only the high priest entered the inner room,

and that only once a year, and never without blood, which he offered for himself and for the sins the people had committed in ignorance ... **When Christ came as high priest** *of the good things that are already here, He went through the greater and more perfect tabernacle that is not man-made, that is to say, not a part of this creation. He did not enter by means of the blood of goats and calves; but* **He entered the Most Holy Place once for all by His own blood, having obtained eternal redemption.** *The blood of goats and bulls and the ashes of a heifer sprinkled on those who are ceremonially unclean sanctify them so that they are outwardly clean.* **How much more, then, will the blood of Christ, who through the eternal Spirit offered Himself unblemished to God, cleanse our consciences from acts that lead to death,** *so that we may serve the living God!"* (Hebrews 9:7-14, NIV).

He did all of this for us! Jesus said, "... ***I have come that they may have life,*** *and that they may have it more abundantly. I am the good shepherd.* ***The good shepherd gives His life for the sheep,***" (John 10:10, NKJV). Jesus gave His life so we could have life!

Today, Jesus Christ is the only one who resides in heaven and He mediates between God and men. *"For there is one God and* ***one mediator between God and men,*** *the man Christ Jesus, who gave Himself as a ransom for all men,"* (1 Timothy 2:5-6, NIV).

■ Don't Insult God

In light of all that we've looked at, can you see it's an absolute insult to compare any past or present religion, religious leader or icon to Jesus Christ? They are not even in the same league. He was the one and only substitute.

Jesus said, *"I am the way and the truth and the life.* ***No one comes to the Father except through Me***,*"* (John 14:6, NIV). He's the only one qualified to make such a statement.

When Jesus died on the cross—in the physical world, it was blood and guts, but when Jesus died on the cross—in the spiritual world, it was life over death.

This is why Jesus really is the only way.

Chapter Seven

■ What About People Who Don't Know?

What about people who have not heard about Jesus? What about the people who live in the remote jungles of the rain forest? What about those in India? China? Antarctica? Outer Mongolia? How could a loving God hold people accountable or send anyone to hell—especially those who haven't heard?

> *Yeah, what about...?*
> *Great questions.*

Let's take a look at this topic, but first we must answer this fundamental question: Is God fair?

■ Is God Fair?

Do you believe God would unfairly judge, declare as guilty or send anyone to hell? If He's God at all, He's not going to be unfair to anyone. Foundationally, this is critical.

Everything we know about God and His character—as revealed in His Word—denotes a God who is just and fair. The Bible says: God is love. He's not a sadist. Masochist. Murderer. Dictator. Tyrant. Terrorist. He is love.

Moses said, *"He is the Rock; His work is perfect.* ***Everything He does is just and fair.*** *He is a faithful God who does no wrong; how just and upright He is!"* (Deuteronomy 32:4, NLT).

> *God is fair.*

OK, so...what about people who don't know?

What about people in remote parts of the world who've never heard of Jesus—what about them? Let's look at three things we know for sure.

■ God Reveals Himself By Instinct

God is fair because He has written His law in every person's heart. The awareness of an Almighty God is intuitive to mankind. It's in our DNA—our wiring. People instinctively call on God in times of trouble. People automatically pray when facing danger—even those who say they don't believe in God find themselves calling out to God! As the old saying goes, "There are no atheists in a foxhole."

Romans 2:14-16 tells us, *"When outsiders who have never heard of God's law follow it more or less by **instinct,** they confirm its truth by their obedience.* ***They show that God's law is not something alien, imposed on us from without, but woven*** *into the very fabric of our creation. There is something deep within them that echoes God's yes and no, right and wrong.* Their response to God's yes and no will become public knowledge on the day God makes His final decision about every man and woman. The message from God that I proclaim through Jesus Christ takes into account all these differences," (MSG).

God has written the knowledge of Himself on the tablet of each person's heart. The way we respond to that knowledge will be made public on the final day.

■ God Reveals Himself In Creation

God is fair because He reveals Himself through His creation.

*"**The heavens tell of the glory of God.** The skies display His marvelous craftsmanship. **Day after***

day they continue to speak; night after night they make Him known. They speak without a sound or a word; *their voice is silent in the* skies; **yet their message has gone out to all the earth, and their words to all the world** ..." (Psalm 19:1-4, NLT).

The very heavens preach of God, the creator! All of creation reveals God.

"For the truth about God is known to them instinctively. **God has put this knowledge in their hearts.** *From the time the world was created,* **people have seen the earth and sky and all that God made. They can clearly see His invisible qualities—His eternal power and divine nature. So they have no excuse whatsoever for not knowing God**," (Romans 1:19-20, NLT).

No excuses.

If people who have never heard of Jesus simply observe the creation and worship the creator, God will be revealed to them.

The Bible tells us, "**Yes, they knew God, but they wouldn't worship Him as God or even give Him thanks. And they began to think up foolish ideas of what God was like.** *The result was that their minds became dark and confused. Claiming to be wise, they became utter fools instead. And instead of worshiping the glorious, ever-living God, they worshiped idols made to look like mere people, or birds and animals and snakes. So God let them go ahead and do whatever shameful things their hearts desired. As a result, they did vile and degrading things with each other's bodies.* **Instead of believing what they knew was the truth about God, they deliberately chose to believe lies. So they worshiped the things God made but not the creator Himself,** *who is to be praised forever. Amen,"* (Romans 1:21-25, NLT).

Notice, this passage tells us that God has revealed Himself through creation; yet if people choose to worship created things rather than the creator and if they exchange the truth of God for a lie; these people won't have any excuse when they stand before God.

It's no wonder the Bible says, *"Let God be true, and every man a liar,"* (Romans 3:4, NIV). God is right and He tells the truth.

■ God Reveals Himself By Giving Grace

God is fair because He reveals Himself by giving us grace—His ability and strength—to believe! The Lord works in us to know and to do His will. He wants everyone to believe. He wants everyone to know His Son Jesus Christ. The Bible tells us, *"... For **it is God who works in you** to will and to act according to His good purpose,"* (Philippians 2:13, NIV).

When God gives us His grace, He enables us to believe. Prior to grace, we are blinded. Once the Lord sheds His grace on us; it's as if our eyes are open and we see things we had not seen. God's grace "greases the wheels" for us to receive salvation. By grace He gives us the ability to have faith in His Son, Jesus Christ.

*"For **it is by grace you have been saved,** through faith—and this not from yourselves, **it is the gift of God**—not by works, so that no one can boast,"* (Ephesians 2:8-9, NIV).

To whom does God give this type of grace gift? A selected few? No! God gives His grace to everyone so that they may believe.

*"For **the grace of God that brings salvation has appeared to all men**,"* (Titus 2:11, NIV).

God is fair and He gives all men the grace that

brings salvation. No one is left out! He gives us the grace we need to have faith and then it's our choice to receive and believe. He won't twist our arm. *"But as many as **received** Him, to them He gave the right to become children of God, to those who **believe** in His name,"* (John 1:12, NKJV).

We all get an opportunity to believe! Everyone gets their time and their chance to make a choice for Jesus Christ.

*"I have seen something else under the sun: The race is not to the swift or the battle to the strong, nor does food come to the wise or wealth to the brilliant or favor to the learned; but **time and chance happen to them all**,"* (Ecclesiastes 9:11, NIV).

There have been debates for centuries over whether God chooses us or we choose God. It seems clear that the answer is: both! God chooses all of us and He gives us the grace to choose Him!

"**For God so loved the world** that He gave His only begotten Son, that **whoever believes in Him** should not perish but have everlasting life," (John 3:16, NKJV).

■ God Reveals Himself By Preaching

God is fair because He reveals Himself through the preaching of the gospel. He has commanded all believers to go into all the world to tell others the good news of the gospel.

Jesus told all of His followers to "Go!"

"Then Jesus came to them and said, 'All authority in heaven and on earth has been given to Me. Therefore **go** and make disciples of all nations, baptizing them in the name of the Father and of the Son and of the Holy Spirit, and teaching them to obey everything I have commanded you. And surely

I am with you always, to the very end of the age,'"
(Matthew 28:18-20, NIV).

Believers have a responsibility to take the gospel
to the ends of the earth so that everyone can hear
the good news of Jesus!

*"**We're Christ's representatives.** God uses us
to persuade men and women to drop their differences and enter into God's work of making things
right between them. **We're speaking for Christ
Himself now: become friends with God; He's
already a friend with you.** 'How?' you say. In
Christ. God put the wrong on Him who never did
anything wrong, so we could be put right with God,"*
(2 Corinthians 5:20-21, MSG).

The bottom line? The Bible is clear. God is love
and He is using all possible means to point people
toward Him and His Son Jesus. God is fair and no

one will have a valid excuse for unbelief when they stand before Him. God will hold us accountable for the knowledge we have.

Now, let's bring this question a little closer to home.

What about you?
Can you claim ignorance?
Have you heard the gospel?
What will you do?
Will you trust Jesus today?

■ Will God Twist Your Arm?

God won't twist your arm! He won't force you or anyone to believe. You have a free will and you may choose to accept or reject Jesus.

There were plenty of people in Jesus' day that didn't believe in who He was. He didn't beg or plead or make them say, "Uncle!"

On one occasion, a group of people who had seen Jesus' ministry in action simply walked away from Him. Jesus didn't chase them down. He turned to the rest of His disciples to see if they wanted to reject Him also. Jesus is willing to let us walk away. He gave us a free will and He lets us use it!

When Jesus asked the crowd if they wanted to leave Him; Peter made a profound statement, ***"Lord, to whom shall we go? You have the words of eternal life.*** *Also we have come to believe and know that You are the Christ, the Son of the living God,"* (John 6:68-69, NKJV).

So, what's the verdict for you? Knowing all of this "Jesus stuff" isn't the point. It's what you do with what you know that's important. What do you do with this information? You respond.

■ God Doesn't Grade On A Curve

Not convinced? You need to be. Before you can make a choice to believe in and receive Jesus Christ, you really need to understand the ramifications if you don't. It's sobering to understand your eternal plight because of sin and the state of spiritual death. Many of us have become very good at rationalizing our sin. We tell ourselves, *"I'm not that bad. Sure, I've **sinned**, but I'm not a **sinner**. Surely, God wouldn't send me to hell. I know a lot of people worse than me."*

There is just one problem with that way of thinking. God doesn't grade on a curve!

God isn't comparing us to others. God grades on a straight scale and in order to pass His muster, you must get 100%. According to God's grading system, the cut off is perfection! Nothing less. If we haven't lived the A+ sinless life, we flunk!

Some people still think God grades on a curve. They figure they'll die, waltz up to the pearly gates and let God know all about their good deeds, religious life, and benevolent intentions. Many will be surprised to learn that they've prepared for the wrong exam! Perhaps it's worth taking a few moments to look at the one question God is putting on His final exam.

God's final exam will have one question: Have you been perfect? The obvious answer is: No!

This is a problem for all of us. *"...The person who keeps all of the laws except one is as **guilty** as the person who has broken all of God's laws,"* (James 2:10, NLT).

*"... For **all have sinned and fall short** of the glory of God,"* (Romans 3:23, NIV).

We've all sinned. If we've broken one of God's laws, we are just as guilty as if we've broken all of His laws! Ever lied? Cursed? Used the Lord's name in vain? Cheated? Stolen? Lusted? Broken one of God's commandments? You're guilty. I'm guilty. We flunked.

Here's the bummer about that: "...**The wages of sin is death**," (Romans 6:23, NKJV). If we have not been perfect, we are guilty as charged and the wage we must pay is death. We've all sinned. We all deserve an "F." We've all flunked.

Get the picture?

The result? Death—an eternal separation from God, unless, we can find a substitute willing to take our place! That's where Jesus comes in. He was our substitute. He came to our rescue.

Jesus lived a sinless life and earned 100% on God's final. He loved us so much, He gave us the gift of His A+! Now, it's up to us to believe and receive.

He chose to pay a wage He did not owe, so we could get a grade we did not deserve. *"For the wages of sin is death, but **the gift of***

God is eternal life in Christ Jesus *our Lord,"*
(Romans 6:23, NKJV).

This is why the gospel of Jesus Christ is called
"good news"!

In fact, the news is so good that when we receive
Jesus Christ, God makes us as righteous as He is!
*"God made Him who had no sin to be sin for us, so
that in Him we might become the righteousness of
God,"* (2 Corinthians 5:21, NIV).

■ The Evidence Is In

The evidence is in and overwhelming! Jesus IS the
only way to God.

The gory, bloody details were necessary for the
salvation of mankind! Jesus has proven Himself
to be our Savior, Redeemer, Lord, Lamb of God,
High Priest, Mediator, Salvation and Substitute.

I trust you've seen the Lord in a new light—not as a mean, narrow-minded, exclusive, intolerant God, but as a good Father God who loves you so much He worked a Master Plan to sacrifice His own Son in order to reverse the curse of sin and death! I pray you've seen Jesus as the hero He is. I am confident that you've seen Him as more than just another religious figure, but as God in the flesh on a rescue mission to save us and give us eternal life! Perhaps you'll want to ponder these verses that reinforce the unique role Jesus holds.

*"**Salvation is found in no one else,** for there is no other name under heaven given to men by which we must be saved,"* (Acts 4:12, NIV).

*"**He has given us eternal life, and this life is in His Son. So whoever has God's Son has life; whoever does not have His Son does not have life.** I write this to you who believe in the Son of God, so that you may know you have eternal life,"* (1 John 5:11-13, NLT).

"What this means is that those who become Christians become new persons. They are not the same anymore, for the old life is gone. A new life has begun! **All this newness of life is from God, who brought us back to Himself through what Christ did.** And God has given us the task of reconciling people to Him. For God was in Christ, reconciling the world to Himself, no longer counting people's sins against them. **This is the wonderful message He has given us to tell others**," (2 Corinthians 5:17-19, NLT).

Jesus is the only way to God.

■ It's Your Choice

You have to make a choice. You must decide to accept or reject Jesus Christ as your Lord and Savior. Knowing about God is not the same as knowing Him, personally.

Some people are under the illusion that living in America makes you a follower of Jesus. It doesn't. Some people think that growing up in a Christian home makes you a believer. Nope. Some are convinced that going to church makes you a Christian. No again. As an old saying goes, "Going to church doesn't turn you into a Christian anymore than going to McDonald's turns you into a hamburger."

Becoming a child of God is not automatic; it's a choice. You have to choose. To accept. To believe. To receive. You have a free will. Choosing Jesus is the response God's looking for.

You must choose on purpose.

Unfortunately, some people respond with indifference and apathy—their choice. Some people respond with unbelief—also a choice.

Some respond with, "Hmmm interesting"—a passive choice. Some respond with "Ah, it's a bunch of garbage!"—a volatile choice. Some people have no response—but a non-response is a choice! Others respond with childlike faith and acceptance—definitely, a choice.

Remember what C.S. Lewis said? *"You must make your choice. Either this man was, and is, the Son of God, or else a madman or something worse. You can shut Him up for a fool, you can spit at Him and kill Him as a demon; or you can fall at His feet and call Him Lord and God. But let us not come with any patronizing nonsense about His being a great human teacher. He has not left that open to us. He did not intend to."*[1]

It's true.

"...To all who believed Him and accepted Him, He gave the right to become children of

God. They are reborn! *This is not a physical birth resulting from human passion or plan—this rebirth comes from God,"* (John 1:12-13, NLT).

Jesus said it simply, *"I assure you, unless you are born again, you can never see the Kingdom of God,"* (John 3:3, NLT).

> *You must be born again.*

Jesus also said, *"I assure you,* ***those who listen to My message and believe in God who sent Me have eternal life.*** *They will never be condemned for their sins, but they have already passed from death into life,"* (John 5:24, NLT).

Don't wait any longer. Believe in and receive Jesus Christ. Confess Him as your Lord and personally invite Him into your life to forgive you of your sins and to give you life, life, life!

■ Final Questions

What is your response? Are you ready to trust Christ and invite Jesus into your life?

"Don't you realize how kind, tolerant, and patient God is with you? Or don't you care? **Can't you see how kind He has been in giving you time to turn from your sin?"** (Romans 2:4, NLT).

"He has given us eternal life, and this life is in His Son. So whoever has God's Son has life; whoever does not have His Son does not have life. *I write this to you who believe in the Son of God, so that you may know you have eternal life,"* (1 John 5:11-13, NLT).

Would you like to pass from death to life? Would you like to know for sure that Jesus is your Lord?

Would you like to know that when you die, you will spend eternity with God in heaven?

"Salvation that comes from trusting Christ ... **For if you confess with your mouth that Jesus is Lord and believe in your heart that God raised Him from the dead, you will be saved.** *For it is by believing in your heart that you are made right with God, and it is by confessing with your mouth that you are saved. As the Scriptures tell us, 'Anyone who believes in Him will not be disappointed.' Jew and Gentile are the same in this respect ...* **'Anyone who calls on the name of the Lord will be saved,'"** (Romans 10:8-13, NLT).

Do you want to be saved? Do you believe that Jesus died on the cross for your sins and was raised from the dead by God? Will you surrender, invite and confess Jesus as the Lord of your life now? If so, let's pray.

Dear God,

"I am so thankful that You did not leave me in my sin and spiritual death. I thank You for sending Jesus to rescue me. Jesus, thank You for coming to earth with Your eternal, sinless blood. I appreciate the gory, bloody details. I believe You are the only way to God and heaven. Thank You for laying down Your life on that cross for me. I am so grateful that You became my substitute and took the punishment I deserved, so that I could have forgiveness and eternal life. You've been so kind and patient with me. Jesus I do believe that God raised You from the dead and today I invite You into my life. Thank You for forgiving all of my sins. I declare that Jesus is my Lord. Help me to know You better and to become the person You created me to be. In Jesus' Name. Amen."

If you prayed this prayer, I encourage you to do three things to get to know Jesus better:

1. Start reading the New Testament.

2. Start talking to Jesus from your heart to His.

3. Start attending a Spirit-filled Bible church.

3 Things.

Study Guide

Conversation Starters

Chapter One

1. Why is it important to be respectful of others' beliefs; while passionate and persuasive about your own?

2. What puts Jesus in a league of His own?

Chapter Two

1. How does God define "life"?

2. How does God define "death"?

Chapter Three

1. What one thing overcomes death?

2. Where is life found?

Chapter Four

1. What type of blood did God need?

2. Why was the virgin birth necessary?

Chapter Five

1. The devil wanted to disqualify Jesus from His mission. Describe the pressures Jesus faced.

2. Why does the cross seem foolish to some?

Chapter Six

1. Describe the role of a "substitute."

2. Share one verse or passage from the Old Testament that predicts Jesus' coming.

Conversation Starters

Chapter Seven
1. Name one way God reveals Himself to man.

2. Why will no one have an excuse when they stand before God?

Chapter Eight
1. What does "God doesn't grade on a curve" mean?

2. Have you made a choice to receive Jesus and confess Him as your Lord? Are you ready to do so today?

Bibliography

Works Cited

Chapter One

[1] *Pew Research Center's Forum on Religion & Public Life*, http://religions.pewforum.org/reports, July 28, 2008.

[2] Ibid.

[3] Ibid.

[4] *USA Today*, http://www.usatoday.com/news/religion/ 2008-06-23-pew-religions_N.htm, July 2, 2008.

[5] *New York Times*, http://www.nytimes.com/2008/06/24/ us/24religion.html?_r=1&hp&oref=slogin, June 24, 2008.

[6] Lewis, C.S. *Mere Christianity*, HarperOne, 2001.

Chapter Eight

[1] Lewis, C.S. *Mere Christianity*, HarperOne, 2001.

Other Resources

Get A Grip Mini-Books: The Question Series

HELL - How could a loving God send anyone there?
DEATH - What happens next? - coming
SICKNESS - What does God think about it? - coming
HEALING - How does God do it? - coming
SUFFERING - Why does God allow it? - coming
WOMEN - What's their role in church? - coming
JESUS - Is He really the only way?

Getting A Grip On The Basics Bible Study Series:

Getting A Grip On The Basics
Getting A Grip On The Basics Of Serving God
Getting A Grip On The Basics Of Health And Healing
Getting A Grip On The Basics Of Prosperous Living
Getting A Grip On The Basics For Kids
Getting A Grip On The Basics For Teens
Getting A Grip On The Basics – Spanish

Bite Sized Bible Studies Series:

Satisfied Lives For Desperate Housewives
Kissed or Dissed
The Friends God Sends
Don't Factor Fear Here
What To Do When You Feel Blue
Grace For The Pace

Bite Sized Bible Studies DVD Curriculum:

Satisfied Lives For Desperate Housewives
Don't Factor Fear Here - coming
Grace For The Pace - coming